The
WEATHER
Project Book

Francis Wilson

Headway · Hodder & Stoughton

Our weather

Planet earth, (which might more accurately be called planet ocean), is something like a spinning cannon-ball shooting through space, surrounded by a thin ring of gases just a fraction of a millimetre deep. We are like the specks of dust stuck to the cannon-ball under the gases.

This ring of gases is really an ocean of air. The air is stopped from flying off into space by the force of gravity pulling it down. Our **atmosphere**—the name given to the ocean of air—is moving all the time. This is because of three things: (1) because the world spins round from west to east once every 24 hours; (2) because mountain ranges stick up into the atmosphere obstructing the flow of the atmosphere; and (3) because the world is heated unevenly by the sun—hot in the middle, cold at the poles.

The constant changes in the atmosphere are what we call the weather. The average weather over many years we call the climate. Someone from another world coming to ours would say the most striking features of our atmosphere are the **jet streams**.

Jet streams are high altitude fast currents of wind that wiggle their way round each **hemisphere**. They form above middle **latitudes** where there are sharp temperature differences because of the overlapping plates of polar and tropical air.

Britain from space

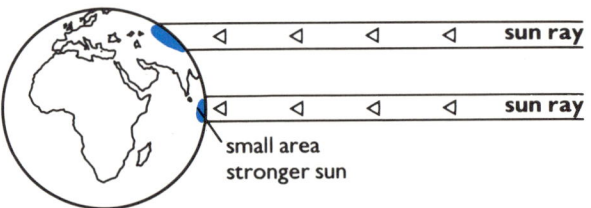

sun ray

sun ray

small area
stronger sun

The sun's rays on the globe

Jet stream

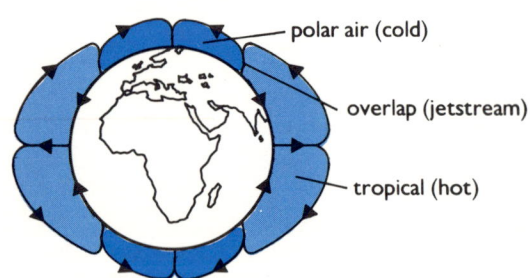

polar air (cold)

overlap (jetstream)

tropical (hot)

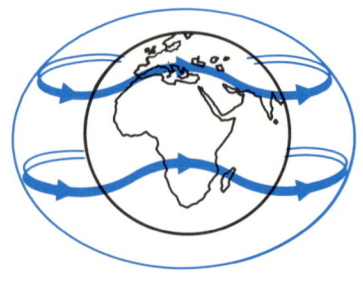

Jet streams circling the globe

Jet streams are very important to us because they steer the weather swirls beneath them, dragging them across continents. For example, a jet stream over Britain typically means lots of unsettled rainy weather being dragged in from the Atlantic Ocean.

Things to find out and do

Air weight
You can show that air has weight by doing this simple experiment. You will need a balloon, a balance, some weights, some plasticine and a pump. Put the empty balloon at one end of a balance and ensure that it is balanced. Use the plasticine if your weights are too heavy.

Now blow up your balloon using a pump, not your breath. Look at your balance and you will see that the balloon end is now heavier and you will need more weight before you can regain balance. High pressure is heavier than low pressure.

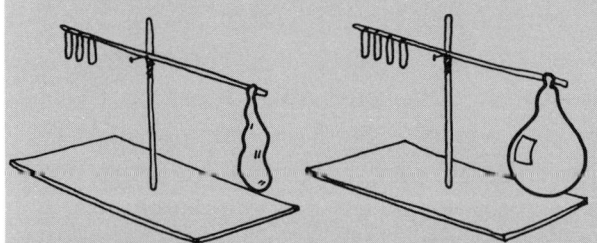

Air pressure
When you drink through a straw you are taking air from the straw. Air pressure pushes down on the top of the liquid and forces it up the straw. If you put your straw in a bottle of drink and then seal the top of the bottle with silver foil (make sure it is airtight) you will find that sucking your drink is more difficult. Do you know why?

air pressure — silver-foil

You can create your own high pressure by blowing up a balloon. What you have inside is high pressure. If you burst the balloon or let the air out in a rush you reduce the pressure and create wind. Wind blows from high pressure to low pressure.

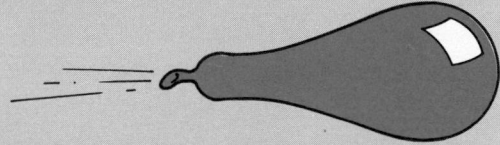

One way of finding out which way the wind is blowing is by simply wetting your finger and holding it up in the wind. It will feel cold on the side from which the wind is blowing. Check with your compass and you will know which is the wind direction.

Wind deflection
Because we live on a rotating planet our wind is deflected. To see this, make a disc out of card the same shape as a 12″ record, with a hole in the centre. Put it on a record turntable and spin it round anticlockwise. Imagine the centre is the north pole and the rim is the equator. Draw a path with chalk from the centre, straight away from you, as the disc spins.

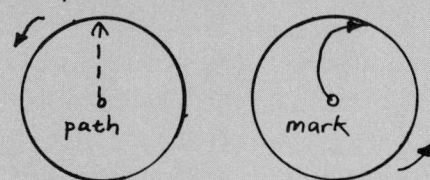

path   mark

The mark of the chalk shows how winds are deflected to the right in the northern hemisphere. Wind spirals out of high pressure regions, and swirls into low pressure areas.

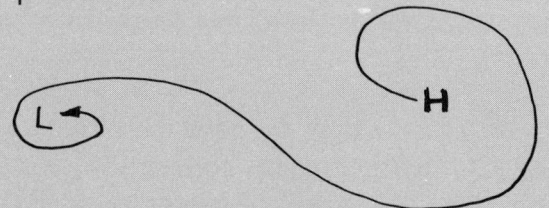

L   H

Clouds

Clouds are made up of floating water droplets that we can see. Usually we cannot see the water in the air, but it is always present, and this is called **water vapour**. When the air is cooled enough, this invisible water vapour drops out **(condenses)** onto tiny bits of dust and salt floating in the air. On cold nights, for example, the surface air drops dew onto the lawn.

However, air most frequently cools when it is forced to rise. As the air rises it expands and this causes the air to cool. The temperature where clouds begin to form in this rising air is called the **dew point**.

There are three reasons why air rises and forms clouds:

1 Where winds blow over land, hills and mountains force the air to rise over them. As a result mountains are often shrouded in cloud and are usually very rainy places.

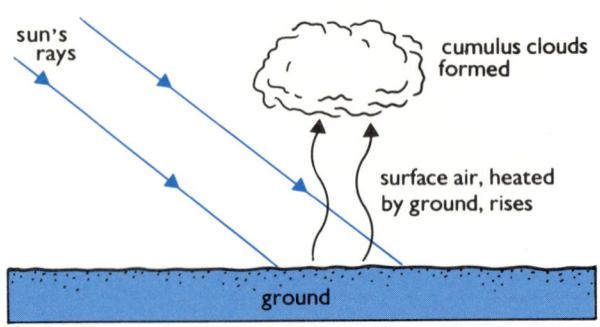

2 On sunny days the ground is heated, which in turn heats the air above it. As hot air rises (by **convection**), so **thermals** form, often taking moist currents of air high enough to be topped by billowing clouds. These can sometimes develop into showers or even thunderstorms. Thermals without clouds are called blue thermals.

3 In the United Kingdom the most important cause of rising air is within the huge weather systems called **depressions**. The large banks of cloud are formed when cold masses of air and warm, moist masses of air battle for territory. The colder, denser air undercuts and forces up the lighter, warmer air. This battleground is known as a **front**. It often gives both heavy falls and long periods of rain over very large areas, sometimes the whole country.

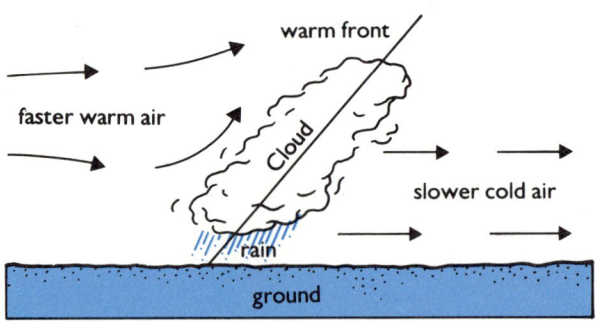

We use Latin words to describe clouds:
  1 CUMULUS means convection (rising hot air)
  2 NIMBUS   means raining or snowing
  3 CIRRUS   means wispy threads
  4 STRATUS means layered
  5 ALTO   means high up

Ten clouds to spot

Name	Shorthand	Appearance
CIRRUS	Ci	Wispy curls
CIRROCUMULUS	Cc	Fleecy, silky sheen; mackerel sky
CIRROSTRATUS	Cs	Thin, milky veil; halo effect on sun
ALTOCUMULUS	Ac	Coarse and fleecy; often in rows
ALTOSTRATUS	As	Light grey veil; weak sun
NIMBOSTRATUS	Ns	Dark veil; no sun
STRATOCUMULUS	Sc	Pancakes or rolling blanket – a wintry grey covering
STRATUS	St	Lifted fog, drizzly grey
CUMULUS	Cu	Heaped separate cauliflowers
CUMULONIMBUS	Cb	Biggest Cu, anvil top, black bottom

Things to find out and do

Write down when and where you spotted the clouds below, and what happened to the weather in the 24 hours that followed.
Cloud base heights are typically 9 000 metres for Ci, Cc, and Cs. For the medium level clouds Ac and As the base is around 3 000 metres. Low cloud heights are Ns 300 metres, Sc 900 metres, St 150 metres, Cu 900 metres, Cb 900 metres.

Ci
∅ When ....
what followed? ....

Cc
○ When ....
what followed? ....

Cs
○ When ....
what followed? ....

Ac
○ When ....
what followed? ....

As
○ When ....
what followed? ....

Ns
○ When ....
what followed? ....

Sc
○ When ....
what followed? ....

St
○ When ....
what followed? ....

Cu
○ When ....
what followed? ....

Cb
○ When ....
what followed? ....

What they tell us

Ci followed by Cc means 'mackerel sky – rain is nigh': rain will come in a day or so.
Cs followed by As means rain will arrive that day.
Ns means it is about to rain.
Sc means the weather is settled, mostly dry.
St means damp and dreary weather.
Cu means bright and cheerful weather: 'Humourous cumulus never gloomerous!' Sometimes the Cu go over the top and produce Cb. That's when the thunder starts!

Colourful sayings

> 'Red sky at night is a shepherd's delight.
> Red sky in the morning is a shepherd's warning.'

A red sky is caused by sunlight passing through a thick layer of air, as happens at dawn and at dusk. When there are clouds in the sky we cannot see this red light. Because of the direction in which the earth spins, our weather normally comes from the west. As the sun also sets in the west, a red sky means that good, clear weather is on the way. In the morning a red sky means that good, clear weather is in the east and passed, so that maybe it is the turn of the bad weather.

> 'A rainbow at night is a sailor's delight.
> A bow in the morning's the sailor's warning.'

You can only see a rainbow when the sun is behind you. So a rainbow in the evening means the rain is to the east – probably going, while the air to the west is clear – probably coming. In the morning the reasoning is turned about.

Things to find out and do

Hot air rises
Make a cone out of paper. Cut around the open end. Hang your cone by a thread over a toaster (only do this experiment with an adult's help) and you will see proof that hot air rises. The experiment will work, though less well, over a radiator.

Gliders use thermals to rise. Can you make some model aeroplanes or gliders out of balsa wood or paper and make use of hot air to fly them?

Condensation

You can use condensation to water your plants or grow some seeds without having to water them.

Put some seeds in a plant pot of compost and cover them with a thin layer of compost. See that your compost is thoroughly damp. Cover the pot with a plastic bag and watch what happens. Where does the water come from? You can water a pot plant in the same way. You can also try this experiment outside by securing a transparent plastic bag over one branch of a tree.

If you can find a large glass or plastic jar (a sweet jar is a good size) you can make a bottle garden which you should never need to water.

Rainbows

See if you can make your own rainbow. You will need a sunny day, a glass of water and a sheet of white paper. Put the glass of water on a windowsill in the sun and the sheet of white paper on the floor below it so that the

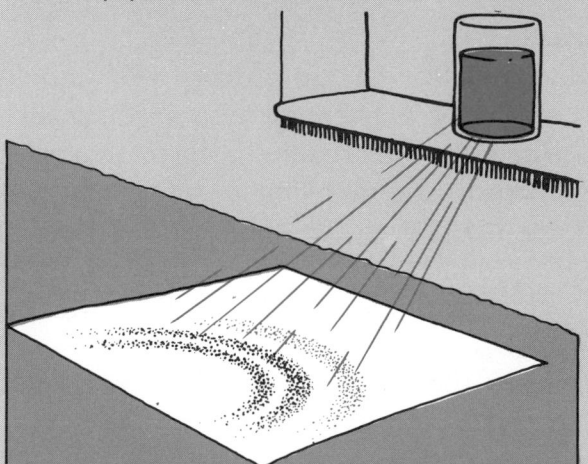

sun shines through the glass and onto the paper. With a little bit of manoeuvring you should be able to get a rainbow on your piece of paper.

If you have a prism you can do the same experiment and be sure of success.

Another way to make a rainbow is out in the garden on a hot day. You will need a hose pipe with a spray nozzle. Stand with your back to the sun when it is fairly low in the sky and spray the hose in a fine spray in front of you. If you aim for something fairly dark like a bush or tree you should see a rainbow.

Windspeed

Windspeed increases with height. It may even change direction! This means that clouds at different levels move at different speeds and directions. To compare speeds on different days and at different levels try using a garden rake.

Go out into the garden and turn your rake so that the clouds are scudding along the tips of the prongs. This shows the wind direction at that cloud level.

To find out windspeed use a stopwatch and time how long it takes individual clouds to get from one side of the rake to the other. If you ring your local Met. Office they will tell you the windspeed at that cloud level. For example, your cloud might have taken 10 seconds to cross the rake, and the official wind speed was 40 mph: note down these times each time you measure and soon you will have a windspeed scale to use with your rake!

Measuring and observing

To fill in the observation book drawn up for you on the inside front cover you need to measure air pressure trend, wind speed and direction, cloud amount and type, visibility, temperature, humidity, and precipitation (rain, hail, and snow).

A **barometer** (you may have one of these at home or school) will show you whether the pressure is rising, falling or steady.

Wind direction is the direction that the wind is coming from. Wind speed can be estimated by observing the movement of such things as smoke and trees, as shown on the **Beaufort Scale**.

Beaufort No.	Description of wind	Effect on land
0	Calm	Smoke rises vertically.
1	Light air	Direction shown by smoke, but not by wind cones.
2	Light breeze	Wind felt on face; leaves rustle; wind cone moved by wind.
3	Gentle breeze	Leaves and small things in constant motion; wind extends flag.
4	Moderate breeze	Raises dust and loose paper; smaller branches are moved.
5	Fresh breeze	Small trees in leaf begin to sway.
6	Strong breeze	Large branches in motion; umbrellas used with difficulty.
7	Very strong breeze	Whole trees in motion; difficult to walk in wind.
8	Fresh gale	Breaks things off trees; very difficult to walk into the wind.
9	Strong gale	Slight damage to buildings; chimney pots and tiles blown off.
10	Whole gale	Trees uprooted; much damage to some buildings.
11	Storm	Widespread damage to trees and buildings.
12	Hurricane	Countryside is devastated.

Cloud amount and type can be judged by eye. Cloud amount is given on a scale from 0 to 8, called **Oktas**. For example:

8 Oktas	Total cloud cover
4 Oktas	Half the sky is covered with cloud
0 Oktas	No clouds in the sky

Cloud types are described in the table on page 5.

To measure visibility a good view is needed. On a clear day note down well-known landmarks, such as a village, a range of hills, a wood, or a TV mast. Use an Ordnance Survey map to find out how far away they are. When you take readings, the furthermost landmark that you can see will give you an estimate of the visibility.

A cheap maximum and minimum thermometer from a garden shop can be used to read the highest and lowest temperature of the day, and also the temperature at time of reading. This should be hung on a north-facing wall to avoid direct sunlight. All temperatures given in weather reports are **shade air temperatures**.

Humidity can be measured by having an extra thermometer called a **wet bulb thermometer** and a set of hygrometric tables (HMSO book).

Precipitation is measured using a rain gauge.

Finally you may want to make some weather remarks about what the weather has been doing.

Most weather instruments are expensive to buy. It is possible, however, to make some of them for next to nothing.

Barometer

Make a **barometer** – a simple device for indicating trends in air pressure: the more the air pushes down, the more the needle of a barometer points up the scale. You will need: a wide mouthed jar, large rubber balloon, drinking straw and glue, thick rubber band, cardboard, needle and plasticine.

Cut off the neck of the balloon, and stretch the rest of it tightly over the mouth of the jar. Slip the rubber band round the neck to keep the balloon in place. Tape the needle to one end of the drinking straw to act as a pointer. Glue the other end of the straw to the centre of the balloon. Do this in a room where the temperature is constant, out of direct sunlight, on a day when the air pressure is around 1013 **millibars** – a middling sort of day (check this in the paper or on the television weather forecasts). Place the card firmly on a plasticine base behind the pointer. The idea is to find out whether the air pressure since the previous observation has risen, fallen, or held steady. Rising pressure means a getting better sort of day, while falling pressure points to rain on the way. A steady pointer means more of the same.

Rain gauge

Make a **rain gauge** – a simple device for measuring how much rain or melted snow has fallen. You will need a straight transparent plastic bottle, a narrow straight jar, and a ruler.

 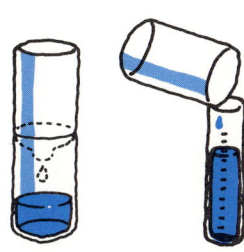

Cut the bottle in half. Use the top half as a funnel, and the bottom half to hold the rain. This ensures the collecting area equals the rain holder area, and none of the rain escapes by evaporation. Using your ruler mark a scale in tens of millimetres on the side of your rain holder. On a day when it pours down all the time, the depth of rain will probably be around 10 mm – surprisingly little. To measure tiny amounts pour 10 mm of water from the rain holder into a tall narrow jar. Mark the level and subdivide the space below it into ten. This gives you an accurate scale in millimetres. On a day when the ground is covered by snow, use the rule that twelve deep of snow melts into one deep of water.

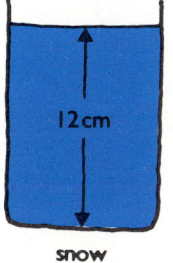 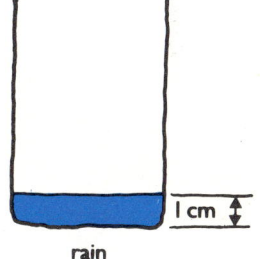

snow   rain

Soil and water temperatures

Fill two pots, one with soil and one with water. Allow them both to come to room temperature by leaving them for several hours in the same room. Then put them both out in the sunlight and leave a thermometer in each one. After one hour look to see which registers the highest temperature. Which warms up quickest, water or soil?

Be a human thermometer

Put your hands into water – one hot, one cold – and keep them there for about a minute. Now put them both into fresh cold water. What do you notice? Do you know why?

Seasons

Annual temperature range and total rainfall

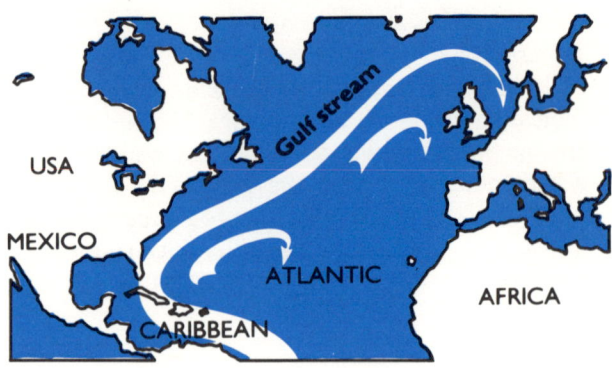

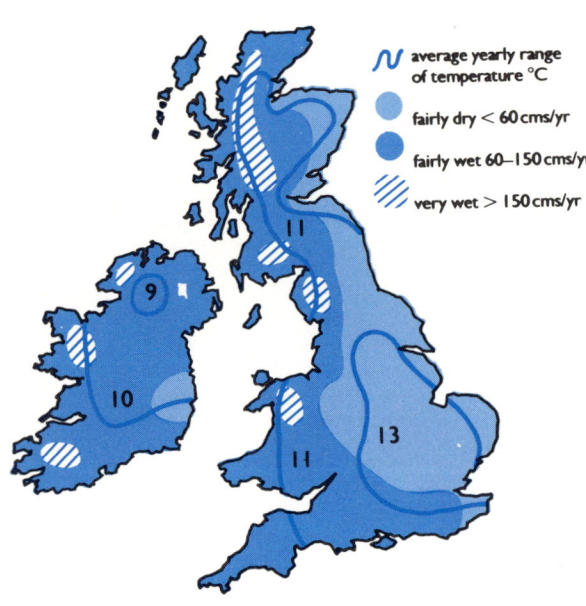

N average yearly range of temperature °C

● fairly dry < 60 cms/yr

● fairly wet 60–150 cms/yr

/// very wet > 150 cms/yr

The map shows Britain divided into two main areas of climate. Over the four seasons eastern Britain has a more continental climate of cold winters and warm summers. Western Britain has a more maritime climate: the winds off the warm Gulf Stream waters keep the winters mild, and feed in cloud. The areas of high rainfall in the west are caused by these clouds meeting the western hills.

The Gulf Stream is a warm current from the Caribbean Sea to Britain that protects us from the extremes of temperature that other places equally far from the equator see most years.

In fact, on average over the year, Britain is the mildest place between the latitudes 50° and 60° north or south of the equator.

Summer

Summer in Britain is when the tilt of the earth's axis is towards the sun, so that the heating is more intense. The seas and atmosphere take some time to warm up, so the summer season is mostly after the summer solstice (the longest day). The farmers' summer is from June to August. At midsummer the sun reaches a height of about 60° in the sky, rising at around 4 a.m. and setting around 8 p.m.

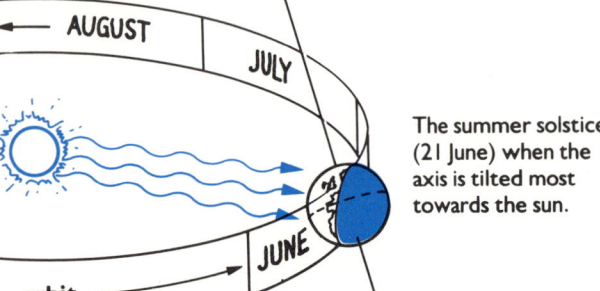

The summer solstice (21 June) when the axis is tilted most towards the sun.

The **Dog Days** of summer (when the Dog Star is rising) loosely refer to days when the shade temperature exceeds 25° C. This normally happens for about ten days each summer, when the air temperature is greater than the skin temperature. It is the combination of hot days, high **humidity** and no wind that gives people the most problems. Humans have some two million sweat glands capable of sweating ten litres every day. We sweat more than any other animal, even the pig (who only sweats on its snout). But if the air is very sticky – approaching 100% **humidity** – the sweat cannot evaporate into the air, so the body cannot lose its excess heat. We overheat. Prickly heat and exhaustion can occur, leading to heat stroke as the body temperature rises.

The highest shade temperature ever observed in Britain was 38° C (100° F) at Tonbridge in Kent on 22 July 1868. The feeling of oppressive warmth on **sultry** days depends on a combination of high temperatures and high humidities, and what one is doing.

Sultry days are not common in Britain. In fact it is claimed that the British summer is three fine days and a thunderstorm!

Things to find out and do

Thunderstorms

Without hills or houses in the way, thunder can be heard up to 18 miles away. However, lightning can sometimes be seen without thunder being heard. This is because of the muffling effect of the clouds. Lightning is a giant spark in which the sudden heating and expansion of the air cause the explosive sound.

Plot the track of a thunderstorm on a map. After a hot sultry spell of weather watch out for rapidly darkening skies. Observe which way the lightning comes from, and start a stopwatch or count immediately. Stop the count when thunder is heard. Draw on a local map a line in the direction of the lightning. The distance to the electrical storm along the line is given by the count between light and sound. One second equals 1100 feet, or three seconds equal 1 km. If subsequent flashes and rumbles have a shorter count, the storm is approaching.

REMEMBER, LIGHTNING KILLS. The electricity there is millions of volts and thousands of amps. It takes only 13 amps to blow a fuse. Stay inside a car or house.

Sunshine

Choose a sunny day for this experiment. Erect a stick on a flat piece of ground. Measure the length of the shadow at hourly intervals through the day. Mark the length each time. What time is the shadow longest? What time is the shadow shortest? Can you work out why the length of the shadow varies?

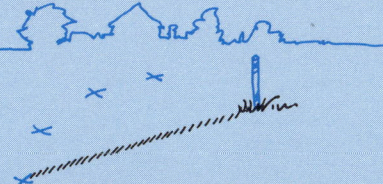

That is how sundials work. There may be one near you in a park perhaps. If you can find one can you tell the time with it?

Evaporation

This is an experiment to find out the drying effect of the sun. All you need is two saucers of water. Put one saucer in the sun, and the other in the shade and see which saucer of water lasts longest. What is happening to the water?

The seas evaporate with the drying effects of the sun so try the same experiment with two saucers of salt water. What are you left with when the water has disappeared?

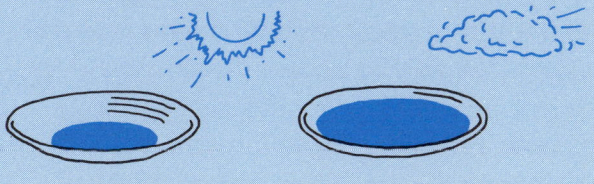

Winter

It is said that the British winter ends in July and starts again in August! This is a huge exaggeration. It can be dull, gloomy and rainy in all seasons but in winter it is always much colder.

The farmers' winter is from December to February. Although December is the darkest month with the weakest sunshine it is usually January and February that are much colder. This is because the summer's heat is stored up in the earth, the air, and especially the sea: this heat is then gradually released during the winter. This particularly helps keeps December mild, even though it has the shortest day (the **winter solstice**) on 21 December.

As Christmas approaches the sun rises at about 8 a.m. and sets around 4 p.m. reaching a height of only 10°. The sun's rays are slanting and spread out thinly, so very little warmth can be felt.

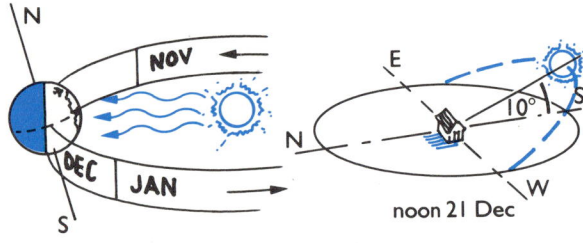

noon 21 Dec

The formation of rain is a complicated process. Almost all rain in our latitudes starts with the freezing of the tiny water droplets in clouds into **ice crystals**. These crystals then bump into each other and join up to form a snowflake until it becomes so big that it falls by gravity. As snowflakes fall they usually melt to become raindrops, but sometimes in winter they land before melting.

As the average winter temperature for Britain is a few degrees above freezing it is very hard to tell whether precipitation will be rain or snow by the time it hits the ground. When the snow wins it is seldom the dry powdery sort that can be blown by snow blowers. Snow-fall when the air temperature is near freezing is the wet snow that brings chaos to roads and railways. The chaos is made worse by the long distances people now travel to work. At Christmas time there is hardly ever snow. Despite the traditional image of snow-covered landscapes and fairs on the iced-up river Thames at Christmas, there has in fact been only one white Christmas in London in the last thirty years, in 1970. The Thames has not frozen over for more than a hundred years, largely because the river is now embanked. This has reduced the width of the river, so that it is deeper and flows faster. One way to avoid pipes freezing up in winter is to keep the water running.

Although on cold clear nights in the middle of winter air temperatures as low as $-27°$ C have been recorded along the Welsh borders, the real killer in winter is **wind chill**. At $-10°$ C, a 20 mph wind will cool you down ten times faster than your body can heat you up. Wind breaks down the cocoon of heat around your body and blows it away. When your body can no longer heat you faster than the wind is cooling you, **hypothermia** begins to bite. Clothing can defend against it, but excessive clothing causes the body to sweat. The sweat acts like damp weather, breaking down the insulating qualities of

the clothing and drawing heat from the body. Some fabrics, such as Goretex*, have billions of holes that are each too small for raindrops to pass, but large enough for sweat to evaporate through. So as long as the wind is not strong this is the best protection against cold weather.

The degree of cold that the wind brings is shown by imagining what temperature it feels like with no wind. The chart shows wind chill equivalent temperatures.

° C air temp	Windspeed mph					
	10	15	20	25	30	35
+3	−2	−6	−8	−9	−11	−12
+2	−3	−7	−9	−10	−12	−13
+1	−4	−9	−11	−12	−13	−14
0	−5	−10	−12	−13	−15	−16
−1	−6	−11	−13	−14	−16	−17
−2	−7	−12	−15	−16	−18	−19
−3	−8	−14	−16	−17	−19	−21
−4	−9	−15	−18	−19	−20	−22

Things to find out and do

Wind chill
On a freezing night put outside two buckets of tap water. Place one out of the wind behind a wind break. Place the other in the wind. Observe when the bucket exposed to the wind begins to freeze over, and time how long after the protected bucket begins to freeze over. The time difference shows the wind chill factor. A different wind the next night will produce a different wind chill factor.

Ice sculpture
In Japan they have a winter festival and competitions are held for ice or snow sculptures. The people make beautiful sculptures of animals, houses and palaces. Ice sculpture is very difficult but you could make very simple ones like this. You will need some plasticine, some small plastic pots (ice-cream pots are good) and a freezer.

Put some plasticine in your pot and make a pattern in it. When your pattern is finished pour in the water and put your mould in the freezer for several hours. When it is frozen you should be able to peel off the plasticine and you will be left with your own ice sculptures – of course it won't last long. If you have any rubber moulds you can make ice sculptures with them in just the same way.

Snowflakes
Most snowflakes have six sides. If you look at some pictures of them you will see that they are very beautiful. Using a hexagon or a circle as a guide make a six sided snowflake pattern. These look lovely done in white chalk on black paper.

Make a cut out snowflake
Using a hexagon as a base fold it and try cutting a delicate pattern. These look particularly good cut out of foil papers.

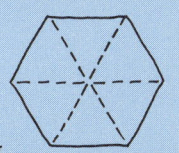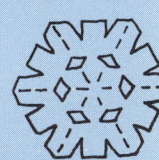

Freezing
When the weather is very cold, pipes in houses can freeze and burst. If you try the simple experiment of half filling a plastic bottle with water, marking where the water comes to and then putting it into the freezer you will see why. Don't try this experiment with a glass bottle – why? What do car owners do about water freezing?

Spring and autumn

During the changeover periods between summer and winter, the earth's axis is tilted sideways to the sun as it circles it. Around September 22 and March 21 sunlight falls equally on the northern and southern hemispheres. The days are the same length as the nights on these dates (the **equinoxes**, from the Latin meaning equal night). The sun rises exactly in the east and sets exactly in the west everywhere.

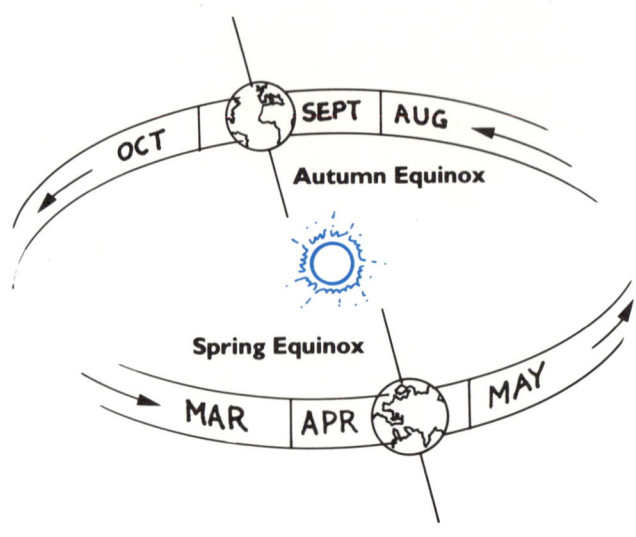

Spring

Spring is the busiest season for all living things. Some say that spring starts on March 21, the spring equinox. Others say that it begins when you can put a foot down on seven daisies all at once. We normally say that the spring months are March, April and May even though the weather takes no notice of such rules!

March
We feel the first warmth from the sun after the winter. There is bustle and excitement everywhere, as birds arrive from overseas to nest, lambs are born in the fields, and the first spring flowers pop up.

April
The uncertain glory of an April day is legendary. A sunny April day will suddenly bring showers, often lasting less than half a hour, with the sun still shining behind them. This is because the land heats up enough to set off thermals. These warm bubbles of unstable air rise through the high level cool air and trigger showers.

Meanwhile the sea temperature lags behind, and is much colder than the warmest masses of air that pass above. This low level air over the sea is cooled to saturation. **Onshore** winds roll sheets of mist and drizzle, called **mizzle**, over the land. This is called **sea fret** in Cornwall, and called **haar** in eastern Scotland.

May
The merry month of May is the month of birdsong, flowers, blossom and greenery. This is a bright, fresh month that can still bring unexpected severe night frost to the valleys, causing damage to flowers, fruit blossom, and vegetables.

May also often sees unexpectedly severe thunderstorms. For example, the Derby Day thunderstorm at Epsom on May 31, 1911 developed lightning that killed 17 people and 4 horses.

Autumn

September

Even after a bad summer, September often brings a spell of fine weather. There is much talk of an **Indian Summer** though this is really a fine spell of weather in October or November in the USA which the American Indians used to store their late crops. In Europe, probably the most reliable spell of good weather (the 'Old Wives' Summer') happens in late September.

October

Sometimes storms occur around September 22, when they are called **equinoctial gales**, but more often October is the rainiest and stormiest month of the year. Often the first real storms of winter turn up towards the end of October. The storm of October 25, 1859, sunk a ship off Anglesey killing 500 people, and destroyed the pier at Brighton. This storm led to the setting up of the **Met. Office**. The storm of October 16, 1987, devastated southeast England, flattening millions of trees and causing total chaos. This storm led to the largest computer in the world being bought for the Met. Office, to give **meteorologists** a better chance to predict such happenings.

November

November is usually the foggiest month of the year. Travelling can be hazardous, especially when **black ice** forms on the roads. Black ice is so called because it is clear rather than fuzzy-looking ice, and so takes on the colour of the road. It is clear because the water freezes slowly, allowing air bubbles to escape.

This dismal month is best summed up by Thomas Hood:

> No warmth, no cheerfulness, no
>   healthful ease,
> No comfortable feel in any member –
> No shade, no shine, no butterflies, no
>   bees,
> No fruits, no flowers, no leaves, no
>   birds, –
> November!

Things to find out and do

Fog

What is fog? What are the dangers of fog, and which areas of our daily life are most affected? Can fog be removed?

Draw a foggy picture. If you use pastels or chalks you can get lovely effects by doing the scene first and then covering the picture with a thin film of white and gently smudging the colours underneath as you do it.

Fogs used to be much worse than they are now – see if you can find out why.

Weather forecasting

Forecasts begin with people all over the world going outside and observing the weather. They take measurements of all the weather elements – temperature, precipitation, pressure, wind, humidity, cloud, and sunshine. These measurements are then gathered together by the special free exchange Global Telecommunications System, and all fed into a supercomputer. In order to forecast what will happen, we must know what is happening worldwide now.

Our first problem is that most of the world is uninhabited. That is why the Great Storm of October 1987 in Britain came as such a shock. Nobody saw it coming because nobody lives in the Atlantic, where it came from. We have to rely on **ocean buoys**, **weather ships** passing planes, automatic unmanned weather stations, **radars** and **satellites** to tell us roughly what the weather is doing now across remote parts of the world. To look at weather at all heights we use **balloon probes** – instrument packs slung under gas filled balloons. As they go up they are tracked by radar and send back measurements of pressure, temperature, wind and humidity. At around ten kilometres high the balloon bursts, and the instruments fall back to earth by parachute.

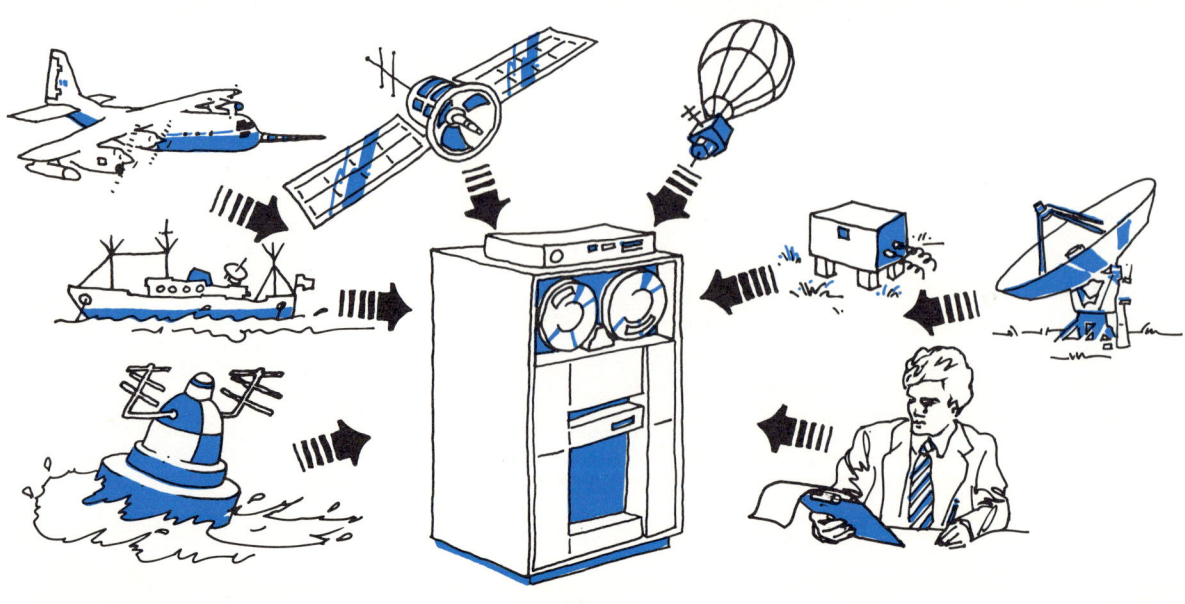

16

World Weather Game

This is a game for two to four players

How to play

Each player has a disc made up of eight segments. There is a picture inside each segment showing one thing that humans are doing that will lead to a weather catastrophe. The aim of the game is to be the first to cover all eight segments by doing something about the problems.

There are three kinds of square that you can land on as you circle the world. The first kind contains pictures of things you can do to help solve the problems. When you land on one of these, match it up with the problem shown on your segment. Cover that segment. For example, if you land on the square with a picture of a fly swat in it, you can cover the picture of the aerosol can up. Each problem and its solution is explained opposite.

The second kind of square contains weather catastrophes. You can't do anything about these — it's too late! When you land on one of these you must pay the price:

A storm surge washes everything away — **put one of your segments back in the middle.**

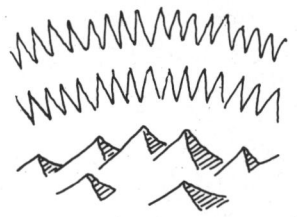

The ice age is here — **put all your segment covers back in the middle.**

The third kind of square has nothing in it. You don't get hit by a catastrophe, but equally you're not getting any nearer to solving the problems!

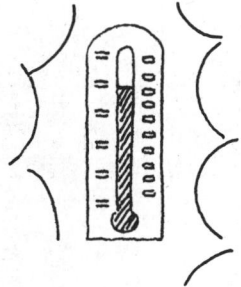

Weather is too hot to move — **lose one go.**

Horrible sunburn — **wait two turns in the shade.**

To start the game

Each player throws the dice: the one with the highest score starts. You only have one throw at each turn. You can start off from any of the empty squares around the globe. You must move in a clockwise direction, following the arrows.

To end the game

The game ends when someone manages to cover a whole disc of segments.

You will need

Four counters, a dice, eight coloured segments each to cover the segments on your discs.

World Weather Game

World Weather Game

Problem	**Solution**

All lights left on in the house waste energy. Electricity produced by coal-fired power stations causes acid rain and the greenhouse effect.

Only use the lights you need. Less waste means less energy has to be produced.

Chopping down rainforests means fewer trees to absorb CO_2. Burning them gives off more CO_2. CO_2 is a greenhouse gas.

Write a letter to the Minister for Overseas Development explaining why rainforests should be preserved. Ask what the government is doing to help.

The gases (CFCs) in many aerosol cans destroy the ozone layer.

Buy a can with an ozone-friendly label, or better still, avoid spray cans altogether.

The energy used to produce all this has been wasted. Rubbish tips give off methane — another greenhouse gas.

Don't buy things you know you'll throw away. Reuse your carrier bags. Why not organise a recycling centre where you live? Paper, glass, and metal can all be recycled.

Burning coal, wood, gas or oil gives off CO_2. Electric fires and heating use up valuable energy, often produced in coal-fired power stations.

Wear a thicker sweater rather than light a fire. Improve the insulation of your house. The key is always to save energy.

Fast food often comes wrapped in foam packaging containing CFCs. Whatever it is made of, the wrapping will be thrown away and wasted. Beef in hamburgers often comes from cattle reared on land cleared by chopping down rain-forests.

Why not try growing your own vegetables instead of eating fast foods? You'll be healthier, and you won't need to package it in plastic! Best of all, do it organically — no fertilisers or pesticides to poison the soil.

Acid rain kills trees and fish. It seeps into the soil and rivers and poisons them. Petrol fumes are a main cause of acid rain.

Get out your bicycle and use it — do you really need a lift to school? Why not cycle? Bicycles don't pollute anything!

Baths use large amounts of hot water, which needs energy to heat.

A shower uses far less water and energy — so if you have the choice have a shower.

The second problem with this observing system is that the observations are unevenly spaced around the world. When these observations are fed into the computer, it tries to make an accurate model of the atmosphere from them. To do this, though, it needs regularly spaced observations, and at regular levels.

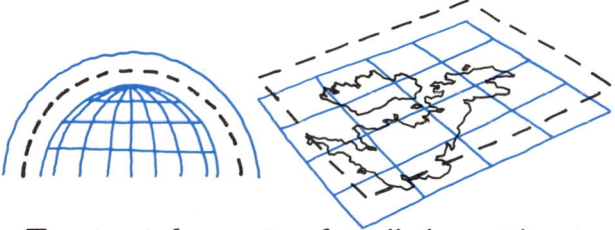

To give information for all the grid points at all the levels, a lot of averaging and guesstimation has to be done.

The resulting snapshot of the atmosphere can then be compared with the previous snapshot to pick out the changes and the trends.

The next step is to use the laws of nature at every grid point. These laws can be written as sums. These sums give us a way of finding out how much a weather element (for example, wind) should change in a short space of time (say 15 minutes). So long as the time step is small, the room for error is small. When the sums have been done for all the weather elements, we have a forecast of the weather over the next 15 minutes. Next we repeat all the sums so as to step forward another 15 minutes. And so on . . .

The supercomputers programmed to do this job are so fast nowadays that they step forward sixty times faster than real time. So after one hour, we have a forecast sixty hours ahead.

The original snapshot that starts the forecast rolling can never be totally accurate – we cannot collect enough data, nor would the computer be big enough to process it all. This means that some errors are bound to slip through the net. So the further ahead the computer forecasts, the more the errors grow. In the end the errors are so big that the forecast is useless. With slow moving settled weather (**high pressure** or **anticyclones**) this is about ten days but with faster moving unsettled weather (**low pressure** or **depressions**) it is only two or three days. When the jet stream is overhead, the forecasts are less accurate. When the jet stream is blocked, the weather moves more slowly and so it is more predictable.

Things to find out and do

Weather forecasting
Do it yourself weather forecasting is limited by what you can see from one place. For example, from a vantage point 25 metres up you can see the horizon 18 km away. High level cirrus 10 000 metres up can be seen above the horizon 200 km away: a typical cloud speed of 40 km per hour makes that 5 hours away. Lone weather forecasting for more than 5 or 6 hours is virtually impossible.

However, it is possible to do better than TV or radio forecasts in the short term by making mental adjustments to the forecast you hear. Do this after examining the sky and using local knowledge about the type of soil, the closeness of hills, the distance to the sea, the direction the valleys run, the lakes and rivers nearby, and height above sea level. Have a go!

Weather forecasts
We all like to hear the weather forecast but there are people for whom it is much more important. Make a list of people whose lives and jobs are affected by the weather.

Farmers
Sailors
Pilots etc.

Weather – news items
Keep a scrapbook of weather stories with cuttings from newspapers, magazines and first hand experiences both in pictures and in writing. You could stick to Britain or include stories from all over the world.

Nowcasting

Nowcasts are very short range forecasts, for one to six hours ahead. They are worked out by looking at what the weather is doing now (using satellite and radar pictures) and continuing the motion into the future at the same speed and in the same direction.

Satellites

The meteorological satellite, **METEOSAT**, hovers 36 000 km over the equator on the **Greenwich meridian**. It orbits the earth once every 24 hours. As the earth turns on its axis once every 24 hours too, this means that the satellite always views the same earth **footprint**.

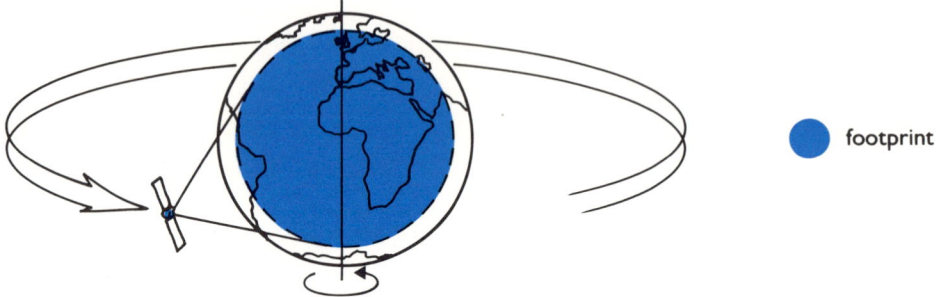

footprint

The pictures that the satellite sends back to earth are made with the help of **radiometers**. These are cameras that pick up the reflected sunlight from the clouds, land or sea – most comes from the clouds and snow cover. Also, the earth gives off heat – **infrared** heat – which shows up the temperature at the top of everything being scanned. This can be used to watch cloud tops – especially at night, when there is no reflected sunlight. The cameras scan the footprint every half hour. By collecting and stacking these **images** on top of each other, like a pack of cards, they can be flicked through to give a movie effect.

In the infrared movie the cold clouds are white, and hot spots like towns are black. In the visible (sunlight) movie the reflective clouds are white, and the oceans are black. The land and sea are stationary and can be outlined. As well as showing which parts of the footprint are covered by cloud, cloud movements reveal what sort of **air mass** is approaching.

Five air masses can be watched by METEOSAT.

Arctic maritime air from the bitter arctic coming in over warmer seas.

Polar maritime air from the cold polar regions coming in over warming seas.

Tropical maritime air from the hot tropics coming in over less warm waters.

Tropical continental air from the hot tropics coming in over dry land.

Polar continental air from the cold polar regions coming in over dry land and the North Sea.

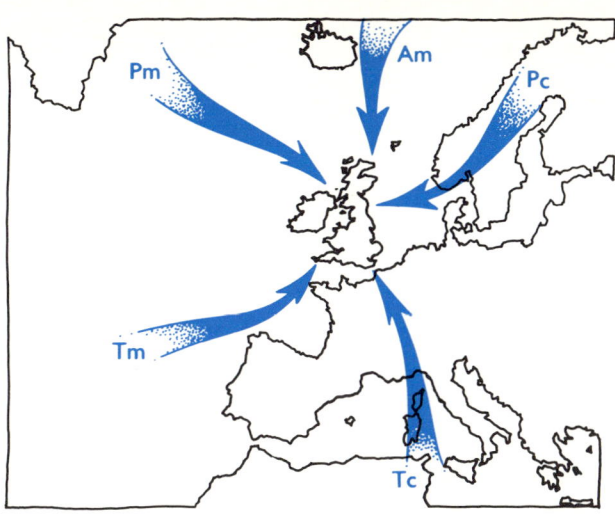

Radar

Underneath the clouds it may be raining. Radar can pick out where the rain or snow is. The radar beam hits the raindrops, and the strength of echo back at the radar scanner tells us how heavy the rain is.

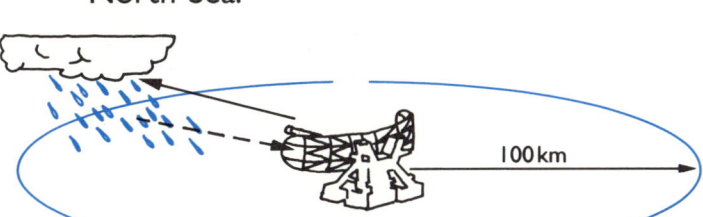

100km

To cover the whole country, a network of radar dishes scans each local area. By joining all the pictures up, a complete radar rain image can be made every 15 minutes. Stacking the images in turn and then flicking through the last few can be used to show, for example, how fast a rainstorm is closing in on Wimbledon Centre Court.

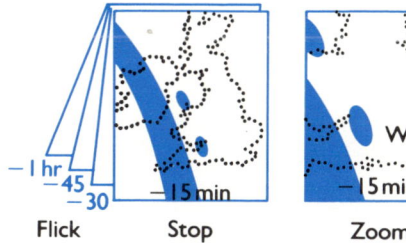

−1 hr −45 −30 −15 min −15 min Now

Flick　　Stop　　Zoom

Things to find out and do

Find a newspaper that each day gives a good report chart of the **highs**, **lows** and **fronts**. (Highs and lows refer to high and low areas of pressure.) Colour polar and arctic air blue (behind the cold fronts), and colour the tropical air red (between the warm and cold fronts). Stack six days' worth and flick through the time-lapse impression of the weather.

Climate and food growth
Different crops like different climates. Where do oranges grow? If you find out you should be able to tell what climate they need to grow. Now try to find out what climatic conditions these foods need to grow:

rice　　　　bananas
tobacco　　pineapples
potatoes

Lifestyle and climate
Some people's lifestyles are governed by the climate in which they live. Bedouins for instance are nomadic because they have to travel around to find water for themselves and their flocks. In the Northern parts of Canada some Inuit (Eskimo) people also lead a nomadic life but this time in search of food.

All around the world people have adapted their lives to the weather. If you look at their homes and buildings you will see this illustrated. In Japan homes are built to withstand earthquake. In Indonesia homes are built of lightweight materials with sides that open to keep them cool. In Siberia homes are built strongly to keep out the cold. Do some illustrations of homes in different climates.

Climate from the beginning

Planet earth is around 4 500 million years old. After the **Big Bang** that created the universe, lumps of boiling debris collided, cooled, and gelled together to form a bald, rocky, erupting planet. It was bombarded by comets and meteorites, and held by gravity in orbit around the sun.

The sun's surface temperature is around 6 000° C. At 92 million miles away this means that primitive earth (once cooled) must have started off with an average surface temperature of −15° C, which swung wildly from day to night.

The atmosphere was started by eruptions from the fiery interior of the earth which gave off gases. These were held to earth by gravity. Volcanoes still throw up this primitive atmosphere of water vapour, carbon dioxide, sulphur dioxide and nitrogen. The primitive atmosphere was rich in the **greenhouse gas** carbon dioxide (for more on this, see p. 22). This is how the average surface temperature of earth came to rise above freezing, to 15° C where it is today. A runaway greenhouse effect, like that on Venus, was stopped by the water steam bursting out of volcanoes and forming huge rain clouds. These washed out much of the carbon dioxide in the atmosphere and formed the oceans. Today the carbon can be found on the ocean beds.

The oceans blocked out lethal **ultra-violet** sunlight, so primitive life began in the oceans. The living cells fed on carbon, and gave off oxygen as waste. Over millions of years oxygen floated up from the oceans into the **stratosphere** to react with sunlight and form **ozone**. Once the ozone shield was thick enough to ward off the lethal ultra-violet rays from the sun, then life moved out from the water's edge onto the land. This changed the planet's surface from bald and reflective to dark and absorbing. This stopped the wild swing of temperature from day to night. Climate and life on earth had become vitally linked. This modern climate began some 500 million years ago. Since then there have been periodic small climate changes called **ice ages**.

Over thousands of years the earth has had a very slow periodic wobble, tilt and spin. It is so small that it is hardly noticeable, but it causes the average surface temperature to change by some 4° C across the globe. Although this does not sound very much, it was in fact enough to reverse the last ice age 10 000 years ago, clearing ice from London, Paris and Chicago back to the pole. Today we are between ice ages; the next one is due within 1000 years, when permanent ice may form as far south as the tarns of Wales and stay for 100 000 years. Whether this will happen or not could be affected by global warming – scientists can't yet tell us.

Things to find out and do

If the world has existed 12 hours, how long do you think man has been around?

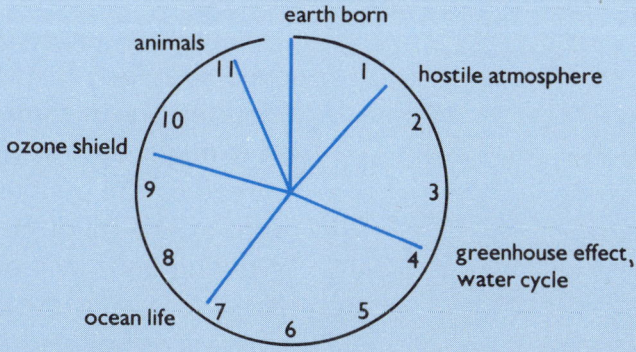

On this scale, by less than a second!

Weather in history
If you look back in history you will find that stories and events have often been influenced by the weather. Noah and his ark is a very obvious one but dig a little deeper and you will find more. The Spanish Armada was destroyed by storms in 1588. Napoleon's invasion of Russia in 1812 was largely defeated by the Russian winter. The Titanic was sunk by an iceberg in 1912. Can you find any other such events? How was weather involved in D-Day, or in the Irish Potato Famine?

Weather gods
In the past people often worshipped weather gods because the weather was so important to their survival. See how many weather gods you can find.

Thor was the Norse god of thunder. Ra or Re was the Egyptian sun god. There are many more – perhaps you could illustrate each one in such a way as to show what he or she is god of. You will find some of them have exciting stories and legends that go with them.

Greenhouse effect

The **greenhouse effect** is the most serious long-term man-made environmental pollution problem facing mankind. Since the industrial revolution the world's population has risen rapidly. As a result, the demand for cheap food and energy has also shot up. To meet the demand, the atmosphere has unwittingly been contaminated with greenhouse gases. The main one of these is **carbon dioxide** (CO_2) from the burning of coal, oil, petrol and gas, as well as from the destruction by burning of the rainforests. This last activity is doubly damaging as trees take in CO_2 from the air, and so help the greenhouse problem. The other greenhouse gases are **methane** from rotting rubbish and cattle, **nitrous oxides** from nitrogen-based fertilisers, and **CFC**s (chlorofluorocarbons) from aerosol sprays and fridges.

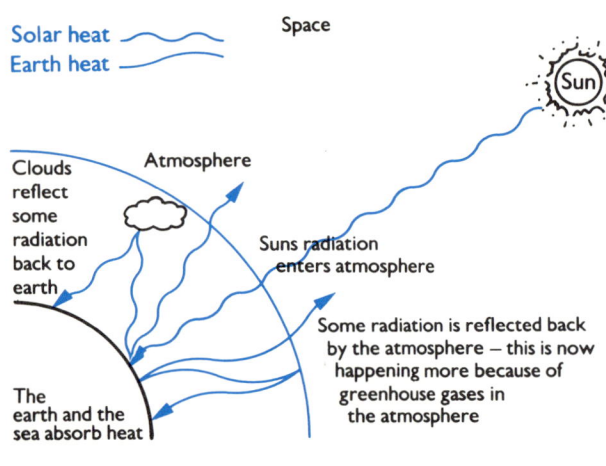

Solar heat —
Earth heat —
Space

Clouds reflect some radiation back to earth

Atmosphere

Suns radiation enters atmosphere

Some radiation is reflected back by the atmosphere – this is now happening more because of greenhouse gases in the atmosphere

The earth and the sea absorb heat

The greenhouse gases allow heat from the sun through to the earth, but block much of the earth's heat from passing back out into space. The trapped extra energy then warms the surface and lower atmosphere. The greenhouse effect has always existed – it preserves life on earth – but man's activities have led to **global warming** on a scale that will bring a major change of climate.

If the pollution continues, in fifty years time southern Britain will have a Mediterranean climate. This is not as good as it might at first sound. Deserts will spread to the middle latitudes of the earth, such as the Mediterranean. The grain-growing belts will be hit by drought year after year. The drought areas will expand polewards because the global warming will be most marked at the poles. This will make the jet streams shift polewards, taking rainy depressions with them.

In fifty years time sea levels will have risen more than one metre. The rise will be due to expanding warmer waters and melting ice sheets. A one metre rise doesn't sound a lot, but what happens when there is a **storm surge** on top of it? The storm surge sends water piling down the North Sea (the **plunger effect**) into the narrow end where the water is deflected to the right. The extra metre and a **high tide** would flood millions of people's homes, and change the coastline of eastern England for ever.

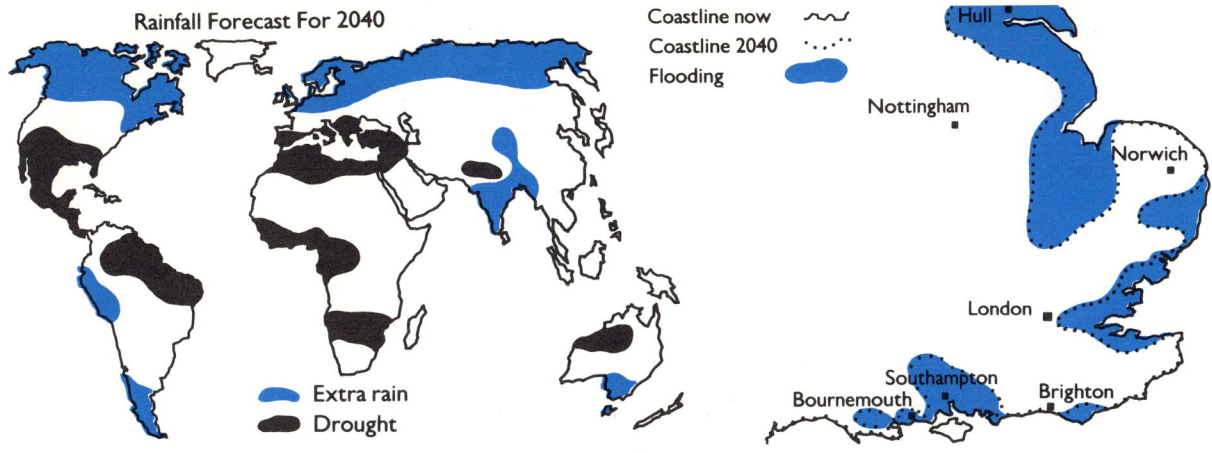

Rainfall Forecast For 2040

Coastline now
Coastline 2040
Flooding

Hull
Nottingham
Norwich
London
Southampton
Bournemouth
Brighton

Extra rain
Drought

In fifty years time we shall have a new climate. What we now consider extreme will by then be the norm. The number of extreme weather events, like hurricanes and droughts, will increase year by year from now on.

Nature tries in two ways to halt the increasing greenhouse effect. Firstly, warmer waters steam off more moisture and form more clouds, which block and reflect the sun's heat and so lower surface temperatures. Secondly, warmer waters breed extra microscopic organisms that feed on carbon dioxide, the main greenhouse gas, and so reduce the greenhouse effect. Just how well nature can contain man-made pollution is not known.

Things to find out and do

Climate changes
Start a scrap book of broadcasts and news cuttings about extreme weather events. Try to establish a pattern connected with warmer climates spreading north.

Greenhouse effect
Gardeners use a greenhouse to trap the heat from the sun. The heat warms up the inside of the greenhouse enabling them to grow things which need heat like tomatoes, cucumbers and sweet corn as well as tropical flowers such as orchids. In a similar way the greenhouse effect is caused when carbon dioxide in the air traps the heat from the sun and makes the air warmer.

You can see what effect a greenhouse can have by putting two thermometers in the sun and covering one with a glass jar. Take their temperatures regularly and you will see your own greenhouse effect.

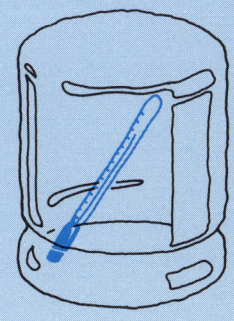

Acid rain

Even if we don't know for sure what the greenhouse effect will bring to the earth, we can already see the destruction caused by **acid rain**. It is killing fish and trees in Canada, Scandinavia, Europe and many third world countries.

All water has things dissolved in it. For example, even tap water contains **nitrates**, poisons which drain into water supplies from fertilisers put on the fields. Rain drops have **sulphur dioxide** and **nitrous oxides** dissolved in them. The sulphur dioxide comes from the chimneys of coal-fired power stations, while nitrous oxides are given off in car exhaust fumes. The chemicals react and eventually produce **sulphuric acid** and **nitric acid**. These acids then fall as acid rain.

Acid is a smelly, sour, burning, stinging chemical. The strength of an acid is measured by a scale of **pH numbers** from 1 to 7.

pH		Example	How many times more acid than neutral
Acid ↑ 1 2 3 4 5 6	strong	lemon acid rain acid lake { rain lake milk	200,000 30,000 4,000 500 60
Neutral 7	weak		0
Alkalis ↓ 8		indigestion tablets	

Scotland and Scandinavia have lakes 400 times more acid than natural, and rain 3 000 times more acid than natural. Although the acid rain starts over industrial areas, the trouble can end up down wind thousands of miles away. The **prevailing winds** usually blow the acid rain Britain produces towards Norway, Sweden, and Denmark.

Trees shrouded in acid mists cannot survive insect attack or disease. Soil washed by acid rain loses its store of essential tree food, and the trees cannot survive frost or drought. In lakes, fish cannot survive a lot of acid pollution, nor can they live with too much contamination by chemicals, such as aluminium. This is eroded into the lakes from the surrounding banks when acid rain falls on them. If the banks or soils are chalky or limestone (weak alkalis), then the rain is made less acid. On the other hand granite and peaty soils are already slightly acid, so the acid is strengthened before entering the water.

Things to find out and do

As one of the major causes of acid rain and the greenhouse effect is the pollution given off by fossil fuels, people are trying to find new sources of energy.

Solar energy
People are beginning to explore ways of using the heat from the sun – solar energy. Do this experiment to find a good way to collect solar energy.

Take two shallow baking dishes, one large and one small – you will find that ones with dark coloured linings work best.

Fill them with the same level of water and cover them with clingflim. Put them on a tray in the sunlight and after 30 minutes take off the clingfilm and take the temperature of the water in each dish. From what you discover you should be able to say whether solar panels need to be large or small if they are to be effective.

Wind power
Can you make a windmill powerful enough to lift a small object? You will need a cork, some stiff card, some strong wire, some plasticine, some thread and some sellotape.

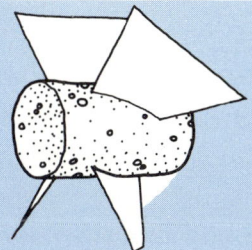

Make blades from the card and insert them in the cork. You may need to use a craft knife so get an adult to help you. Place your cork windmill on a piece of stiff wire and fix this to a piece of wood. Balsa wood is easy to pierce and if firmly fixed will work well. Fix a piece of thread to the wire between the cork and the wood. Secure it with sellotape. Try blowing on the cork – the thread should go up. Gradually add weight to the thread until you get it to lift an object – say a pencil or a piece of plasticine. When you have got to this stage you need to try your working windmill out in the garden or playground – find the windiest spot you can.

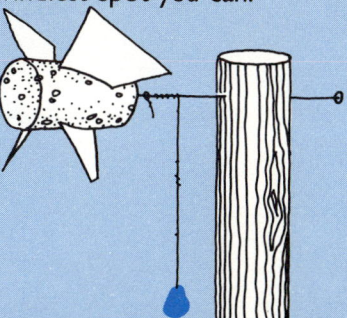

You may find you can make something similar from a construction set. Would increasing the size of the windmill increase the weight it could lift?

Ozone loss and harmful sunshine

To sit in the sun feels good, but we know now that too much sun can be bad for you. This is because the ultra-violet (UV) rays in sunlight can cause skin cancer and failing eyesight.

The sun's UV rays are spread over three ranges. **UVA** triggers skin tanning. **UVB** causes sunburn, and excessive UVB can cause skin cancer. **UVC** causes mutations and cancer of the skin by killing the **DNA** molecules there. Normally UVC and some UVB is prevented from reaching people by the **ozone shield** high in the stratosphere.

The ozone shield is today being thinned by **chlorine**. One chlorine atom can destroy tens of thousands of ozone molecules. Chlorine is released in the stratosphere by CFCs (chlorofluorocarbons). CFCs are produced on the ground by refrigerators and air conditioners, foam packaging, and spray aerosols.

CFCs take years to float up into the stratosphere. However, some CFCs attach themselves to specks of sand floating in the air and are then rained out into the oceans. While airborne they absorb the earth's heat rays: CFC is a strong greenhouse gas making up 20% of the present day greenhouse effect. CFCs are the baddies common to the two separate problems: the greenhouse effect and ozone depletion. In fact above both the Poles, holes in the ozone shield have recently been discovered. This is because virtually all stratospheric cloud occurs only over the poles, and CFCs break down the ozone shield only on the surface of stratospheric cloud droplets.

Ozone can be produced at ground level by direct sunlight reacting with the fumes from car exhausts. This ozone is a shield from harmful UV – but at a price. This ozone is often trapped in a stagnant pool of summertime haze called **photochemical smog** that causes shortness of breath, nausea, and distressing nose, throat, and eye reactions.

Posters

Make a poster to encourage people to buy aerosols that are ozone friendly.

Make a poster to persuade drivers that unleaded petrol is best. Remember that people only glance at posters and your message should be immediately apparent. Don't put too many words on them – try to make their impact very quick.

Weather crossword

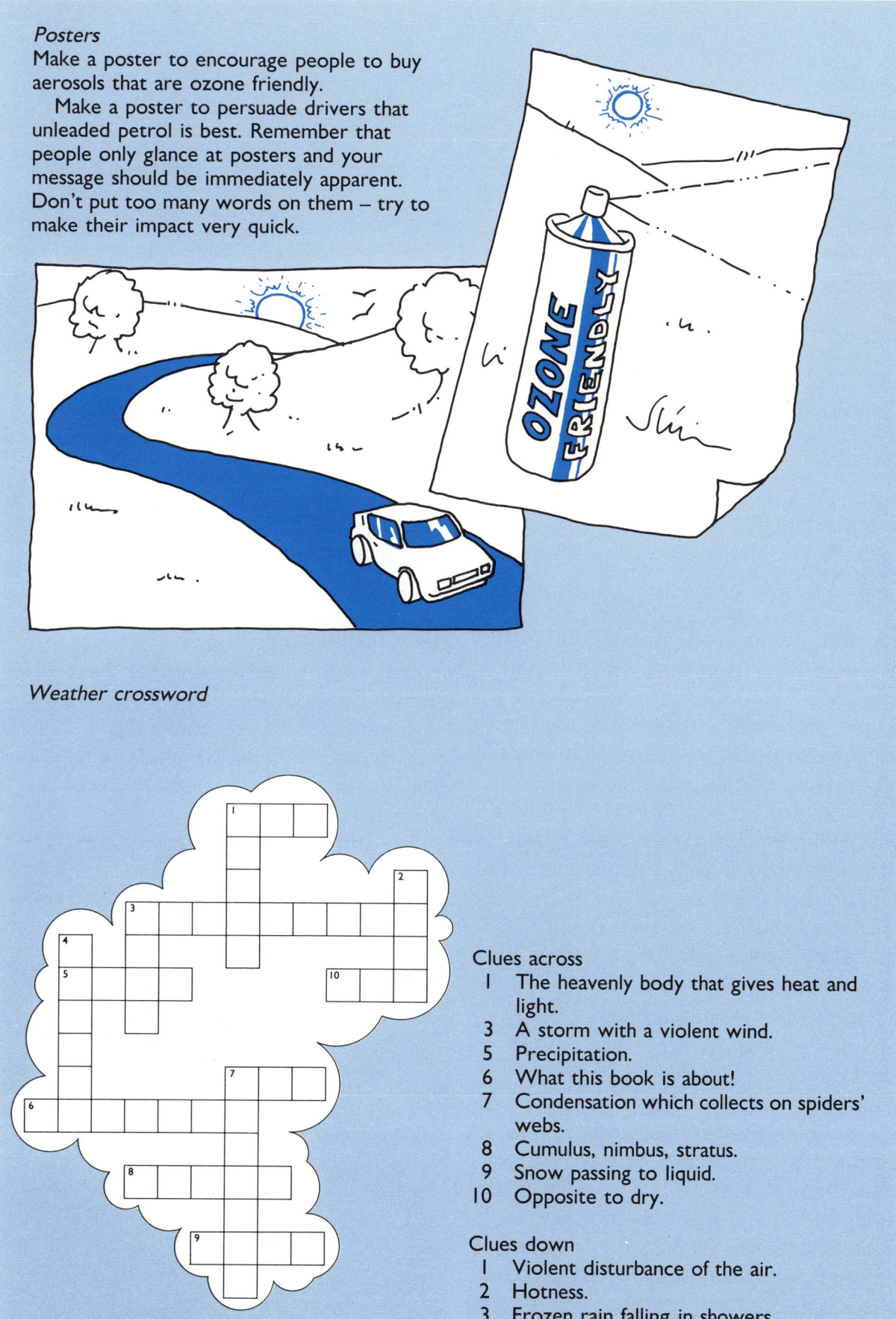

Clues across
1 The heavenly body that gives heat and light.
3 A storm with a violent wind.
5 Precipitation.
6 What this book is about!
7 Condensation which collects on spiders' webs.
8 Cumulus, nimbus, stratus.
9 Snow passing to liquid.
10 Opposite to dry.

Clues down
1 Violent disturbance of the air.
2 Hotness.
3 Frozen rain falling in showers.
4 What a lake does in very cold weather.
7 Continuous dry weather.

Catastrophes and disasters

The trail of devastation left across southeast England on 16 October 1987 was caused by an exceptional storm; an example of a **weather disaster**. By contrast, it was a **weather catastrophe** that wiped out the dinosaurs 65 million years ago, after they had dominated the planet for 130 million years.

Could such a climatic catastrophe happen again? We have to look at clues like these:

1 Although fossils have been found, no life now exists at all in the central Antarctic.

2 For ice sheets to spread rapidly over the entire earth's surface, there would have to be a temperature drop of around 20° C in a few months.

3 The largest volcanic eruption ever recorded (Tambora, Indonesia 1815) blasted 1400 m of mountain into the stratosphere. 1816, known as the year without a summer, or 'eighteen hundred and froze to death', led to thousands of people dying of cold and starvation.

4 The minor eruption of Mt St Helens (USA 1980) caused daytime temperatures to be depressed 8° C as the great ash trail spread out in the sky.

5 Craters on the moon are proof that **asteroids** (minor planets) must have hit this corner of the universe.

6 In Italy and Denmark high concentrations of **iridium** (rare on earth, but common to asteroids) have been found.

By examining the clues, scientists have calculated that a climatic catastrophe will occur if an asteroid 10 km or more wide strikes earth. The speed of collision would release more energy than any nuclear explosion. It would turn a chunk of the earth's crust into hot gas, shooting it right up above the weather, into the stratosphere. Unable to be rained out, the dust cloud would stay for years, reflecting the sun's heat back out to space while allowing earth's heat to escape. Temperatures on earth would plummet. Added to this, the shock of the impact would trigger major eruptions. Volcanic dust and sulphur dioxide released near the equator would rapidly envelop both hemispheres. Surface air temperatures in just two months would drop as much as 40° C across the interiors of continents. Combined with little or no light, crops would fail completely. Around the coasts intense monsoonal storms would rage because of the sharp temperature differences between the continents and oceans. As with the dinosaurs, humans would become extinct.

The smoke from forest fires can have the same catastrophic results. The smoke from a forest fire in Alberta (1950) took just two days to cover the whole of

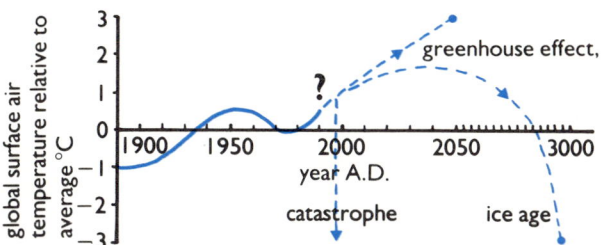

nuclear winter would kill off whoever was left after the war.

The graph shows recent temperature trends worldwide, and offers three very different futures.

Although we cannot control infrequent natural catastrophes such as volcanoes erupting or asteroids colliding with the earth, we can control our own activities.

Canada. Streets had to be lit at midday. In Britain the plume caused a blue moon. Although smoke plumes do not reach the stratosphere (instead they are eventually rained out), smoke particles are much finer than volcanic ash. This makes them much better at scattering the sun's heat back to space, while allowing the earth to cool even more. Therefore very many large and uncontrolled fires burning for months on earth would cause the same climatic catastrophe as an asteroid strike.

The fires left burning after a **nuclear war** would turn out to be even more catastrophic than the blasts, fires and ionising radiation of the war itself. The

We can stop the use of CFC gases, we can control the destruction of the rainforests, we can minimise the burning of fossil fuels: we can do a great deal to reduce the damage we are inflicting on the earth.

We hope that nature's own self-balancing forces will correct our past mistakes and give us time to change to a more weather-friendly way of doing things. This way our future children can enjoy living on the earth with the mostly reasonable weather that we have today.

Things to find out and do

Reporting weather
Make a front page for a tabloid newspaper on an imaginary weather disaster. A flood, a hurricane, a motorway pile up in the fog, any story you like. You will need illustrations as well as written accounts and should try to include some personal dramas as well as the facts and figures of your imaginary catastrophe.

Hurricane names
The weather authorities give alphabetical names to hurricanes. They used to use just female names but now they use male names as well. Make a hurricane alphabet like Hurricane Albert, Hurricane Bertha . . .

Weather stamps
If you are a stamp collector you may like to try and get together a collection of weather stamps. You will find that many countries have issued them.

Musical weather
Using a variety of instruments can you make weather sounds: the drip-drop of the rain, the rumble of thunder, or the crack of lightning? A group of children working together may be able to make a 'storm symphony'.

Weather log book

	Reading 1	Reading 2	Reading 3
Date	1 Jan	2 Jan	3 Jan
Time	0800	0815	0755
Pressure trend	↗	→	↗
Wind — Speed	3	2	4
Wind — From	SW	W	NW
Cloud — Oktas	8	8	4
Cloud — Type	Ns	St	Cu
Visibility	poor	misty	good
Temperature °C — Now	4	6	0
Temperature °C — Max	6	7	0
Temperature °C — Min	3	4	-1
Humidity %	100	95	75
Precipitation since last observation (mm)	2	0.5	3
Weather remarks	rain	drizzle	snow

The Atmosphere

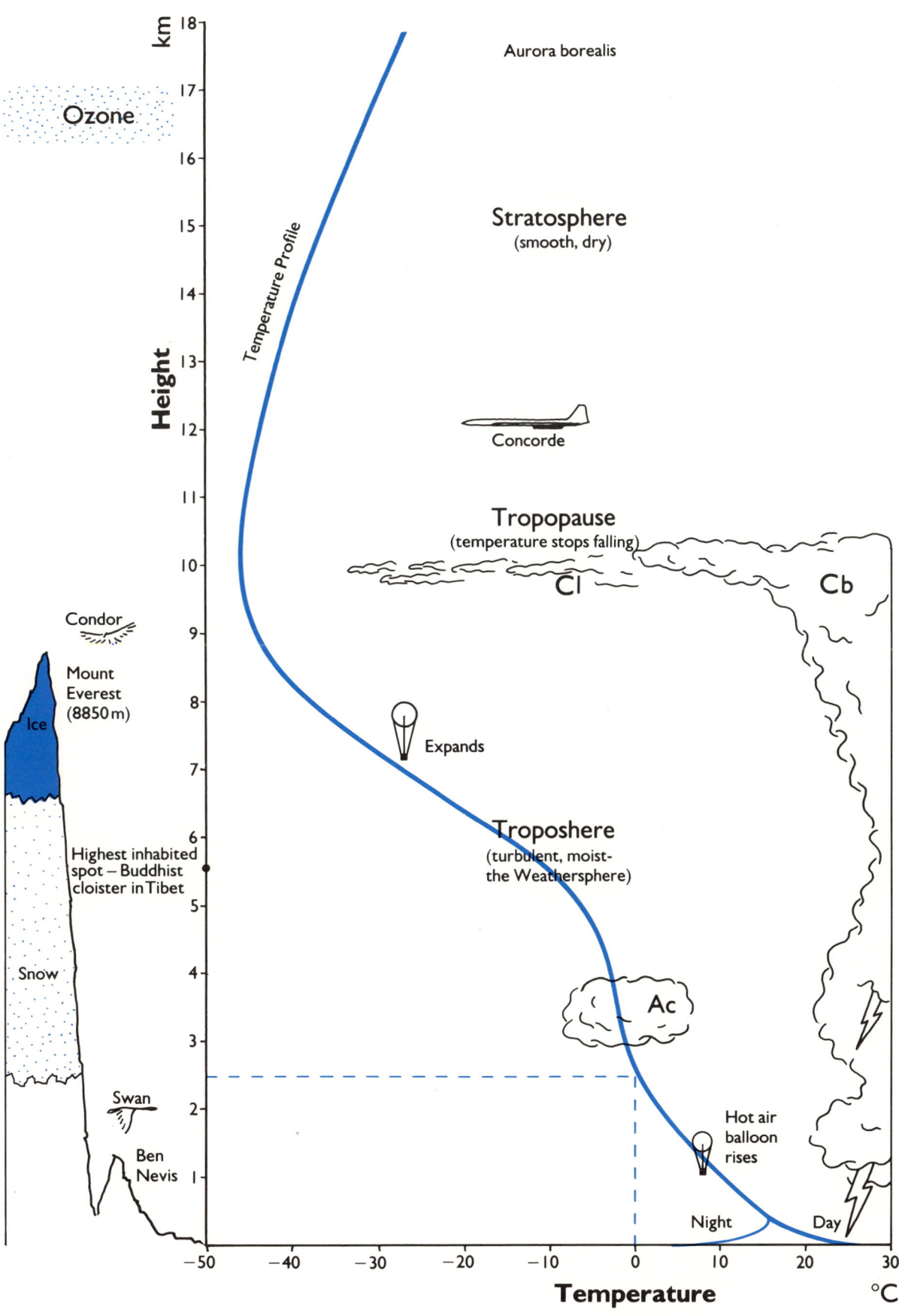

Aurora borealis

Ozone

Stratosphere
(smooth, dry)

Concorde

Tropopause
(temperature stops falling)

Cl

Cb

Condor

Mount
Everest
(8850 m)

Ice

Expands

Troposhere
(turbulent, moist-
the Weathersphere)

Highest inhabited
spot – Buddhist
cloister in Tibet

Snow

Ac

Swan

Hot air
balloon
rises

Ben
Nevis

Night

Day

km

18

17

16

15

14

13

12

11

10

9

8

7

6

5

4

3

2

1

Height

Temperature Profile

−50   −40   −30   −20   −10   0   10   20   30

Temperature

°C

Acknowledgments

The author and publishers would like to thank the following for their kind permission to reproduce photographic material:

University of Dundee Satellite Station (photo 1, p2); Professor Richard Scorer (photo 2, p2); Dr J T Bartlett/Met. Office (photo 3, p5); Chris Streatfeild (photos 4, 5, 8, 9, 10 and 12, p5); C J Richards/Met. Office (photo 6, p5); G A Clarke/Met. Office (photo 7, p5); Angela Murphy/Science Photo Library (photo 11, p5); Keith Kent/Science Photo Library (photo 13, p11); Jerome Yeats/Science Photo Library (photo 14, p12); Gore (photo 15 and use of the Goretex* trademark, p13); Chris Streatfeild (photo 16, p14); Bracknell Times 1987/Met. Office (photo 17, p15); Andrew McClenaghan/Science Photo Library (photo 18, p15); Met. Office (photo 19, p16); European Space Agency (photos 20a, b and c, p18); Professor S Lowther/Science Photo Library (photo 21, p20); Tim Malyon/Science Photo Library (photo 22, p22); Western Mail & Echo Ltd (photo 23, p23); John McMaster/Science Photo Library (photo 24, p24); John Walsh/Science Photo Library (photo 25, p24); Zindler/Greenpeace 1984 (photo 26, p25); Barnaby's Picture Library (photo 27, p26); Martin Black/Barnaby's Picture Library (photo 28, p26); NASA/Science Photo Library (photo 29, p28); Forestry Commission (photo 30, p29).

Answers to the crossword on p. 27:
Across: 1 sun   3 hurricane   5 rain   6 weather   7 dew   8 cloud   9 thaw   10 wet
Down: 1 storm   2 heat   3 hail   4 freeze   7 drought

ISBN 0 340 51378 0
First published 1989

Typeset by Oxprint Ltd, Oxford
Printed in Great Britain for Hodder and Stoughton Educational, a division of Hodder and Stoughton Ltd, Mill Road, Dunton Green, Sevenoaks, Kent by Eyre & Spottiswoode Ltd, Margate, Kent.